ISBN 978-1-332-19197-0
PIBN 10296210

1 MONTH OF
FREE
READING

at
www.ForgottenBooks.com

By purchasing this book you are eligible for one month membership to ForgottenBooks.com, giving you unlimited access to our entire collection of over 700,000 titles via our web site and mobile apps.

To claim your free month visit:

www.forgottenbooks.com/free296210

THE
ROYAL
HOSPITAL
AT
CHELSEA

Price: One Shilling Net.

AN IN-PENSIONER.

IN SUBSIDIUM ET LEVAMEN, EMERITORUM
SENIO, BELLOQUE FRACTORUM, CONDIDIT
CAROLUS SECUNDUS, AUXIT JACOBUS
SECUNDUS PERFECERE GULIELMUS ET
MARIA REX ET REGINA,—MDCXCII.

(Inscription over the Colonnade in the Centre Court of the Hospital.)

I.—ORIGIN AND PURPOSE OF THE HOSPITAL.

THE standing or Parliamentary Army of England was formed in the year 1660. From that time, therefore, dates the system of enlisting men as professional soldiers in the service of their Country for the best portion of their lives, and the consequent obligation on the part of the Country to make some provision towards their general support in old age.

The necessity for national action on behalf of the welfare of veterans as a class had thus arisen. But, as is so often the case, lack of money was an obstacle, and it was not until some years after the Restoration of Charles II. that an ingenious Minister, Sir Stephen Fox, the Paymaster-General of the Forces, devised in 1681 a plan for obtaining the amount, about £160,000, requisite for the purchase of land and erection of a hospital or home for old soldiers. This sum was raised by making, in return for certain concessions, deductions from the allowances granted for army clothing

---

* The word is used in its original meaning—a place for the entertainment of guests.

985907

and accoutrements, by requiring the contribution from the officers of the army of a day's pay in the year, and also by deducting certain sums from the proceeds of the sale of their commissions. In addition the King appealed to the public for voluntary aid, but the appeals were not successful, and the whole of the voluntary contributions amounted only to about £20,000, to which the King added nearly £7,000, an unapplied balance of Secret Service money. The ROYAL HOSPITAL may, therefore, be said to have been partly built by the Army itself, and the larger portion of its lands, including Burton's Court, and about half of the South Grounds which face the Embankment, was also purchased with the funds obtained in this manner. But the Ranelagh Gardens and the eastern portion of the South Grounds were bought with moneys bequeathed by private benefactors. The Hospital, then, is in no sense a charity ; and its inmates, who are ex-soldiers of good character, disabled by wounds or old age, are there in enjoyment of honest independence, earned by meritorious devotion to the service of their Country.

There can be no doubt that it was at first the intention to provide a home sufficiently large to accommodate all veterans who fulfilled the conditions necessary to obtain admission to the Hospital. And when the foundation stone was laid in 1682 the estimate of space was fairly formed to provide for about 500 pensioners. By the time, however, of the completion of the building ten years later, the expectants had grown in number; and when it was opened it was found, therefore,

VIEW FROM RIVER.

(about 1695.)

VIEW FROM KING'S ROAD, 1694.

PORTICO, CENTRE COURT.

necessary to give an *Out-Pension* to those whose admission had to be deferred. Thus arose the system of out-pensions, and the rapid and continuous increase of the Army soon led to the out-pensioners becoming by far the larger body. .

The out-pensioners then, are ex-soldiers who receive an allowance in cash on account of services rendered to the State, while the veterans, known as the in-pensioners, who are accommodated in the Hospital, and number 558, relinquish this allowance, but are provided with uniform, food, furniture, medical attendance, and a small sum as pocket money. When in full dress the in-pensioners still wear in the summer a cocked hat and red frock coat, similar to those used in the earliest days of the Hospital; but knee breeches, stockings and shoes have now been replaced by trousers and boots.

II.—OBJECTS OF INTEREST TO VISITORS.

Visitors are admitted to certain portions of the Hospital at the hours shown on the notice boards. The Services in the Chapel are also open to the public on Sundays, but the accommodation for visitors is limited, and the Chapel is closed to visitors when the service has commenced.

The architect of the Hospital was the famous Sir Christopher Wren, under whose supervision it was erected. Subsequently Robert Adam, who was Clerk of Works to the Commissioners of the Royal Hospital from 1765 to 1792, made certain important alterations in the building, amongst which was the sashing of the windows in the long wards and residences. Sir John Soane, who was Clerk of Works from 1807 to 1837, was also responsible for certain additions to the buildings

The main building comprises the Centre Court, which is enclosed on the east and west by the two wings, and on the north by the Chapel and Great Hall.

Each of the wings contains eight long wards in which the in-pensioners live. Each ward is named after a Governor of the Hospital, those in the west wing being called after the Governors who held the rank of Field-Marshal, those in the other wing after the Governors who were Generals. The arrangements of the wards, which are finely wainscotted with old oak, are all identical. Each is split up laterally into two parts by a corridor. On one side of each half ward is a line of windows, and on the other, in the centre, is a fire-place, on either side of which are the bunks or cubicles of the pensioners, the cubicles nearest to the fire-place being naturally considered the best ones by the old men. A cubicle somewhat resembles a small ship's cabin, and, in addition to a door, has a shutter on a hinge and curtains which give privacy to the occupant. The oak staircases which lead to the wards of the upper storeys are very fine in their dignified plainness, and the rake of the steps, is particularly easy, Wren having in mind that they were for the use of veterans.

A bronze statue of King Charles II. stands in the middle of the Centre Court, the Monarch being attired

4

A LONG WARD.

STAIRCASE, WEST WING.

MARCH PAST, FOUNDER'S DAY, 1921.

A*

COLONNADE.

as a Roman warrior, crowned with the wreath of a victor, and without moustache so that his face may be in keeping with his dress.

This statue, which is the work of Grinling Gibbons, and is one of the few that celebrated carver ever modelled, was the gift of Tobias Rustat, a gentleman of the Court of King Charles, who was one of the early benefactors of the Hospital. On Restoration Day, the 29th May, popularly called Oak-Apple Day, the great Festival Day of the Hospital, when the in-pensioners parade in their full uniform in honour of the founder, King Charles's statue is covered with oak boughs in memory of his escape from Cromwell's troopers by hiding in an oak tree at Boscobel, after the battle of Worcester in 1651.

A stately portico faces King Charles's statue, and on either side of this portico runs a colonnade, the wall of which is partly wainscotted with old oak, while on and above portions of the wainscotting are memorial brasses and other tablets.

The portico leads into a square vestibule paved with stone, and with trophies of flags on its walls, while above these may be seen the cipher of King James II. in moulding ; and from this vestibule flights of stone steps lead eastwards into the Chapel, and westwards into the Great Hall.

The Chapel and the Hall have the same measurements, each being 198 ft. long and 37 ft. wide. The Chapel is panelled with old oak and has a handsome carved and pillared altar screen, and fine altar gates of carved lime wood, much of the carving being by Emmett, chief carver to King Charles II. The centre of the reredos is occupied by a panel of polished wood brought from Jerusalem, the figure upon it representing the Star of Bethlehem. There is also a carved case for the organ, which stands in the Musicians' Gallery. An interesting fresco of the Resurrection, painted by Sebastian Ricci, is on the domed ceiling above the altar.

Certain changes have from time to time been made in the seating in the Chapel and in the position of the pulpit and reading desk, but there has now (1920) been a reversion to the arrangement, as regards the seating, which was adopted by its architect, Sir Christopher Wren, who placed the benches longitudinally.

Many captured standards hang in the Chapel. Those of particular interest are a reproduction of an eagle belonging to the 8th French Regiment, which is placed just below the Musicians' Gallery. The original eagle, which was either of gilt bronze or gold, while the wreath round the eagle's neck was of pure gold, was captured at Barrosa by the 87th Foot (the Royal Irish Fusiliers) under Major Gough, afterwards Sir Hugh Gough. In April, 1852, someone entered the Chapel by a trap door in the roof, and carried off the eagle and banner and staff. Stripping off the eagle and colour, the thief threw away the staff, which was subsequently found and put again in its old position. There is near the altar the flag of the 105th French Regiment, captured at Waterloo by Captain Kennedy Clark of the Royal Dragoons, which has on it as " honours," Jena, Eylau,

CHAPEL.

CHAPEL.

GREAT HALL.

Eckmuhl, Essling, and Wagram. There are also two French Republican flags taken in Egypt, on which are inscribed the words " Discipline et Soumission aux Lois Militaires," two colours of a Prussian regiment in the French service in Spain, and also the eagles of the 62nd and 22nd French Regiments captured at the Battle of Salamanca. Five old staffs, three of which are but bare poles, rags of silk hanging to the others, were captured in Marlborough's great victory at Blenheim. Two of the American flags were taken at Bladensburg in 1814, and of the others three were captured in 1812.

The communion plate of the Chapel of the time of James II., and engraved with his cipher, is extremely handsome, the salvers and flagons and chalices, and the two great candlesticks, being remarkable for the beauty of their shape and workmanship.

The Great Hall, which was used up to the year 1814 as the dining hall of the Hospital, but is now a recreation room, is also wainscotted in oak to the level of the windows, and has a handsome Musicians' Gallery. At its far end there is a dais on which the high table was placed where the officers used to sit at meals. The buttery-hatch is behind one of the panels, and the tables now used for games are those on which the meals were formerly served to the in-pensioners.

Above the panelling of the dais is a large fresco of Charles II. on horseback, with the centre court of the Hospital in the background. The King is depicted as trampling on figures representing treason and anarchy, while round him are other figures emblematic of the happiness and prosperity resulting from his reign. This painting was commenced by Antonio Verrio, a Neapolitan artist, whose work was much in fashion in the reign of Charles II., and finished by Henry Cook. Round the walls are hung portraits by famous painters of Kings George I. and George II., and of Queens Charlotte, Caroline and Victoria; and also of the Duke of Wellington and other distinguished soldiers. And there is an able copy of Sir G. Kneller's portrait of Sir C. Wren, the architect of the Hospital. On the panelling at the western end of the Hall are prints of members of the Royal Family, which were presented to the Hospital, and at the eastern end are other prints and photographs of the Governors of the Hospital, with four exceptions, since its foundation. As in the Chapel many standards captured in past wars are fixed to the walls of the Hall. The most interesting is that on the screen below the great picture of the " Battle of the Standard," the well-known painting by R. Ansdell, R.A., which hangs in the Gallery. The eagle and flag are those of the 45th French Regiment taken by Sergeant Ewart of the Scots Greys at Waterloo, where Ewart not only killed the bearer of the standard, but, in addition, a lancer and a foot-soldier. At the foot of the screen, also, is Sergeant Ewart's sword in a glass case. Near the pictures of the Governors there is a portrait in oils of William Hiseland, an in-pensioner who was 110 years old when this was painted; and below it are leather " black-jacks " formerly used as beer jugs, and glass cases, which contain medals, pewter ware once

THE TERRACE, SOUTH FRONT.

employed in the Hospital, and other objects of interest.

The table on which the Duke of Wellington lay in state in the Hall, after his death in 1852, stands against the screen. On this is placed one of the warrants for the foundation of the Hospital signed by King Charles II., and also the instructions issued in 1692 to the Chaplain. The latter are given under the signatures of certain Commissioners, who then, as now, administered the Hospital, one of those signing this paper being Sir Christopher Wren. On the panels, on either side of the door, are lists of the benefactors who have made gifts of money or in kind to the Hospital.

The public are permitted to enjoy access during certain hours of the day to the grounds of the Hospital, with the exception of the courts enclosed by the buildings, which are reserved for the use of the veterans, and the terrace gardens, with their broad gravel walks, flower beds, old gateways and trophies of cannon captured in Britain's wars. The Ranelagh Gardens, once the famous pleasure gardens of the times of the Georges, are now a stretch of lawns, shady trees and thickets, but the site of the Rotunda, or music and ball room of old days, is still marked by a rise in the ground.

In the Hospital cemetery, which was closed in 1855 for burials, are many interesting memorials and inscriptions. There is the grave of W. Hiseland, the veteran mentioned above, who died in 1732 at the age of 112; that of Doctor Burney, author of the History of Music, who was Organist of the Royal Hospital,

Chelsea, from 1783 to 1814, and was buried in the cemetery ; that of Colonel Chudleigh, Lieut.-Governor of the Hospital from 1715-1726, and father of the notorious Elizabeth Chudleigh, Duchess of Kingston ; and that of William Cheselden, the famous surgeon, who was Surgeon of the Hospital from 1737-1752.

The Infirmary which stands in ground to the west of the main building of the Hospital, is the place of comfort to which the old men retire when they are sick or weak through old age, and here they can only be visited by permission of the Medical authorities. The greater part of this building was erected in 1811, but the oldest portion is of historical interest, having been the residence of Sir Robert Walpole, afterwards Earl of Orford, who was Prime Minister from 1721-1742. The ward shown on the photograph was formerly Sir Robert's drawing-room.

INFIRMARY WARD.

CPSIA information can be obtained
at www.ICGtesting.com
Printed in the USA
BVOW06s1832130817
491956BV00004B/29/P